# Rangers Football Club Quiz Book

## 101 Questions To Test Your Knowledge Of The Most Successful Football Club In The World

Published by Glowworm Press
7 Nuffield Way
Abingdon OX14 1RL

## Rangers Quiz Book

This book contains one hundred and one informative and entertaining trivia questions about Rangers Football Club.

With 101 questions, some easy, some more challenging, this entertaining book will test your knowledge and memory of the club's long, successful and eventful history. The book is packed with information and is a must-have for all loyal Rangers supporters. You will be quizzed on players, legends, managers, opponents, transfer deals, trophies, records, honours, fixtures and more. Enjoyable and educational, this Rangers Quiz Book will provide the ultimate in entertainment for Rangers FC fans of all ages, and will test your knowledge and prove you know your Rangers trivia.

# 2021/22 Season Edition

# FOREWORD

When I was asked to write a foreword to this book I was honoured.

I have known the author Chris Carpenter for a number of years and his knowledge of facts and figures is phenomenal.

His love for football and his talent for writing quiz books makes him the ideal man to pay homage to my great love Rangers.

This book came about as a result of a challenge in a pub!

I do hope you enjoy the book.


Stewart McDonald

Let's kick off with some relatively easy questions.

1. When were Rangers founded?
   A. 1871
   B. 1872
   C. 1873

2. What is Rangers nickname?
   A. The Gers
   B. The Growlers
   C. The Grumblers

3. Who has made the most appearances for the club in total?
   A. Dougie Gray
   B. John Greig
   C. Sandy Jardine

4. Who has made the most League appearances for the club?
   A. Sandy Archibald
   B. Simon Archibald
   C. Steve Archibald

5. Who is the club's record goal scorer?
   A. Ally McCoist
   B. Bob McPhail
   C. Jimmy Smith

6. Who has scored the most penalties for the club?

A. Jimmy Fleming
B. Johnny Hubbard
C. Derek Johnstone

7. Who is the fastest ever goal scorer for the club?
A. Gordon Durie
B. Barry Ferguson
C. Kenny Miller

8. Who or what is the club mascot?
A. Boris Bear
B. Broxi Bear
C. Roxi Bear

9. What is the highest number of goals that Rangers has scored in a league season?
A. 114
B. 116
C. 118

10. What is the highest number of points that Rangers has won in a league season?
A. 96
B. 99
C. 102

OK, so here are the answers to the first ten questions. If you get seven or more right, you are doing very well, but the questions will get harder.

A1. Rangers were founded in February 1872 and the club was one of the 11 original members of the Scottish Football League.

A2. The most common nickname of the club is The Gers although they are also known as The Light Blues and The Teddy Bears.

A3. John Greig is the club's longest serving player and he made a grand total of 755 appearances for the club between 1961 and 1978. Legend!

A4. Whilst John Greig made 498 appearances in the League, Sandy Archibald is the man who made the most League appearances for the club - 513, covering the years 1917 to 1934.

A5. The club's record goal scorer is of course Ally McCoist who scored a total of 355 goals for the club between 1983 and 1998.

A6. The player who has scored the most penalties for the club is Johnny Hubbard who played for the club between 1949 and 1959. He scored 65 spot kicks from 68 taken, 22 consecutively and he became known as the "Penalty King".

A7. Gordon Durie is the fastest ever goal scorer for the club, scoring just 11 seconds after kick off against Dundee United on 1st April 1995.

A8. The club mascot is of course Broxi Bear. He is a brown bear with blue inner ears and nose. He is a popular mascot who enjoys goofing around before home games.

A9. The highest number of league goals scored in a season by Rangers is 118 goals in 38 games during the 1933/34 season. The highest number of league goals scored in a season by Celtic is 116 during the 1915/16 season.

A10. Rangers achieved an incredible 102 points during the record breaking 2020/21 season.  This comfortably beat the previous record of 97 points set during the 2002/03 season.

OK, let's have some questions about the ground.

11. Where does Rangers play their home games?
    A. Ibrox Park
    B. Ibrox Stadium
    C. Rangers Stadium

12. What is the stadium's capacity?
    A. 50,178
    B. 50,781
    C. 50,817

13. What is the home end of the ground known as?
    A. The Broomloan Road Stand
    B. The Copland Road Stand
    C. The Govan Stand

14. What is the club's record attendance?
    A. 114,567
    B. 116,567
    C. 118,567

15. What is the name of the road the ground is on?
    A. Broomloan Road
    B. Copland Road
    C. Edmiston Drive

16. Which stand has the biggest capacity?

A. Broomloan Road (West)
B. Sandy Jardine (North)
C. Main (South)

17. What is the size of the pitch?
    A. 101 x 64 metres
    B. 103 x 66 metres
    C. 105 x 68 metres

18. How many times has the ground hosted
    the Scotland national side?
    A. 14
    B. 16
    C. 18

19. Which of these is a well-known pub near
    the ground?
    A. The Ben Nevis
    B. The Louden
    C. The Real McCoy

20. When did Simple Minds play a memorable
    concert at Ibrox?
    A. 1976
    B. 1986
    C. 1996

Here are the answers to the last block of questions.

A11. Rangers play their home games at Ibrox Stadium, its official name since 1997. The ground was known as Ibrox Park from 1899 to 1997.

A12. The current stadium has an all seated capacity of 50,817; which is the third largest football stadium in Scotland.

A13. Although each stand is normally full of home fans, traditionally the home end of the ground is known as the Copland. Think of it the same way as The Kop at Anfield and the Stretford End at Old Trafford etc.

A14. Although many people say the actual attendance was higher, the stadium's highest *official* attendance is 118,567 for an Old Firm match against Celtic on 2nd January 1939. This is the record attendance for any league match played in Britain.

A15. The stadium's official address is 150 Edmiston Drive.

A16. The Bill Struth Main Stand (the south stand) is the largest of the stands at the ground, with a capacity of 27,000, all seated.

A17. The pitch dimensions are 105 metres long and 68 metres wide, which is 114.8 yards long and 74.3 yards wide.

A18. Ibrox has been a home venue for the Scotland national football team 18 times. The ground most recently hosted a Scotland game in October 2014 when Scotland beat Georgia 1-0 in a UEFA Euro 2016 qualifying match.

A19. The Louden Tavern is one of the closest boozers to the ground being just a few minutes' walk away. It is more than a pub, it is an institution. Be prepared to queue for a pint though.

A20. Simple Minds performed a memorable concert live at the stadium in 1986. Tickets cost £11.50.

Now we move onto some questions about the club's records.

21. What is the club's record win in any competition?
    A. 12-0
    B. 13-1
    C. 14-2

22. Who did they beat?
    A. Blairgowrie
    B. Whitehill
    C. Both Blairgowrie and Whitehill

23. What is the club's record win in the League?
    A. 9-0
    B. 10-0
    C. 11-0

24. Who did they beat?
    A. Aberdeen
    B. Dundee
    C. Hibernian

25. What is the club's record win in European competition?
    A. 8-0
    B. 9-0
    C. 10-0

26. Who did they beat?
    A.  Valencia
    B.  Valerenga
    C.  Valletta

27. What is the club's record defeat?
    A.  0-6
    B.  0-7
    C.  0-8

28. Who was the oldest player to make their
    debut for Rangers?
    A.  Alec Hill
    B.  Clint Hill
    C.  Craig Hill

29. Who is Rangers' oldest ever goal scorer?
    A.  Jim Forrest
    B.  Dave McPherson
    C.  David Weir

30. Who has scored the most hat tricks for
    Rangers?
    A.  Jimmy Fleming
    B.  Ally McCoist
    C.  Bob McPhail

Here are the answers to the last set of questions.

A21. Rangers' record victory is 14-2.

A22. Rangers actually managed to win 14-2 on two occasions! They beat Whitehill on 29th September 1883 and the Gers also beat Blairgowrie by the same score on 20th January 1934.

A23. Rangers' record League victory is 10-0.

A24. The club's record 10-0 League victory was against Hibernian way back on 24th December 1898.

A25. Rangers's record win in European competition is incredibly 10-0.

A26. Rangers beat Valletta, from Malta, 10-0 at home in the European Cup Winners Cup on 28th September 1983.

A27. On 30th April 1937, Motherwell beat Rangers 8-0, the worst defeat in the club's long history. It may have been a long time ago but it still stings.

A28. The oldest player to make their debut for the club is Clint Hill who was aged 37 years and 274 days when he started in a League Cup match against Anna Athletic on 19th July 2016. He went on to make 32 appearances for the club.

A29. David Weir is the oldest player ever to score for the club - aged 38 years and 183 days when he scored against Kilmarnock on 9th November 2008.

A30. Rangers' all time record goal scorer also scored the most hat tricks for the club. Ally McCoist scored an incredible 28 hat tricks in his time at the club.

Her are some trophy related questions.

31. How many times have Rangers won the League?
    A. 51
    B. 53
    C. 55

32. How many times have Rangers won the Scottish Cup?
    A. 29
    B. 31
    C. 33

33. How many times have they won the League Cup?
    A. 21
    B. 24
    C. 27

34. How many times have the club won a major European trophy?
    A. 0
    B. 1
    C. 2

35. When did the club win their first League title?
    A. 1890/91
    B. 1892/93
    C. 1894/95

36. When did the club win their first Scottish Cup?
    A. 1890
    B. 1892
    C. 1894

37. When did the club win their first Scottish League Cup?
    A. 1946
    B. 1947
    C. 1948

38. Who was the last captain to lift the League trophy?
    A. James Tavernier
    B. David Weir
    C. Steven Whittaker

39. Who was the last captain to lift the Scottish Cup?
    A. Christian Dailly
    B. Sasa Papac
    C. David Weir

40. Who was the last captain to lift the League Cup?
    A. Steven Davis
    B. Kyle Lafferty
    C. David Weir

Here are the answers to the latest set of questions.

A31. Rangers has won the League an incredible 55 times. This is a world record.

A32. Rangers has won the Scottish Cup 33 times, most recently in 2009.

A33. Rangers has won the Scottish League Cup 27 times.

A34. Rangers have one major European Trophy in its history - the European Cup Winners Cup back in 1972.

A35. Rangers won their first League title way back at the end of the 1890/91 season.

A36. Rangers won their first Scottish Cup in 1894, the first of many.

A37. Rangers won their first Scottish League Cup in 1947. The competition was only introduced the season before.

A38. The last captain to lift the League trophy was James Tavernier, at the end of the fantastic record breaking 2020/21 season. He lifted the trophy on May 15th 2021 after the last game of the season, over two months after the club were declared champions.

A39. The last captain to lift the Scottish Cup was David Weir, on the 30th May 2009.

A40. The last captain to lift the League Cup was once again David Weir, when he lifted the trophy on the 20th March 2011.

I hope you're having fun, and getting most of the answers right.

41. What is the record transfer fee paid?
    A. £10 million
    B. £12 million
    C. £14 million

42. Who was the record transfer fee paid for?
    A. Mikel Arteta
    B. Tore Andre Flo
    C. Barry Ferguson

43. What is the record transfer fee received?
    A. £7 million
    B. £8 million
    C. £9 million

44. Who was the record transfer fee received for?
    A. Carlos Cuellar
    B. Alan Hutton
    C. Trevor Steven

45. Who was the first Rangers player to play for Scotland?
    A. Isaac McMahon
    B. Jacob McNab
    C. Moses McNeil

46. Who has won the most international caps whilst a Rangers player?
   A. Ally McCoist
   B. Kenny Miller
   C. David Weir

47. Who has scored the most international goals whilst a Rangers player?
   A. Ally McCoist
   B. Bob McPhail
   C. Kenny Miller

48. Who is the youngest player ever to represent the club?
   A. Barry Ferguson
   B. Derek Ferguson
   C. Duncan Ferguson

49. Who is the youngest ever goalscorer?
   A. Sandy Jardine
   B. Lee McCulloch
   C. Willie Thornton

50. Who is the oldest player ever to represent the club?
   A. Jim Forrest
   B. Dave McPherson
   C. David Weir

Here are your answers to the last set of questions.

A41. In November 2000 Rangers paid Chelsea £12 million for a striker.

A42. Rangers' record transfer fee paid out was for Norwegian striker Tore Andre Flo.

A43. In January 2008 Rangers received £9 million from Tottenham Hotspur for a defender.

A44. Rangers' record transfer fee received was for Alan Hutton.

A45. The first Rangers player to be capped by Scotland was Moses McNeil who made his debut in March 1876 against Wales.

A46. Ally McCoist won the most international caps whilst a Rangers player – being capped 60 times whilst at the club. Kenny Miller and David Weir both won 69 caps for Scotland in total, with Miller winning his caps whilst at a number of clubs and Weir winning a number of his caps whilst an Everton player.

A47. Ally McCoist has scored the most international goals whilst a Rangers player – scoring 19 time for Scotland whilst he was with the club.

A48. The youngest player ever to represent the club was Derek Ferguson who made his debut aged 16 years and 24 days against Queen of the South on 24th August 1983.

A49. Willie Thornton is the club's youngest ever goal scorer. He scored aged just 16 years and 312 days playing against Arbroath on 9th January 1937.

A50. Centre back David Weir holds the record as being the oldest player to represent Rangers. He played against Malmo on 26th July 2011 aged 41 years and 77 days.

I hope you're learning some new facts about the club.

51. Who is the current chairman?
    A. James Blair
    B. Paul Murray
    C. Douglas Park

52. Who is the club's longest serving manager of all time?
    A. Walter Smith
    B. Bill Struth
    C. William Wilton

53. Who started the 2021/22 season as manager?
    A. Pedro Caixinha
    B. Steven Gerrard
    C. Graeme Murty

54. How many League games did Rangers win in the 2020/21 season?
    A. 30
    B. 31
    C. 32

55. Which of these songs commemorates a memorable European match?
    A. Wimbledon Town
    B. Wolverhampton Town
    C. Workington Town

56. Which of these is a Rangers fanzine?
    A. Follow Follow
    B. Ibrox Talk
    C. One Team in Glasgow

57. What animal is on the club crest?
    A. Leopard
    B. Lion
    C. Tiger

58. Where is Rangers training ground?
    A. Bishopbriggs
    B. Lennoxtown
    C. Milngavie

59. Who are considered as Rangers' main rivals?
    A. Alloa Athletic
    B. Celtic
    C. Partick Thistle

60. Which of these is a song associated with the club?
    A. The Benny Boys
    B. The Billy Boys
    C. The Bobby Boys

Here are the answers to the last set of questions.

A51. Douglas Park holds the title of chairman, having taken up the position in March 2020.

A52. Bill Struth is the club's longest serving manager of all time. He held the position from May 1920 to June 1954 and was in charge of a staggering 1,179 matches.

A53. Steven Gerrard started the 2021/22 season as manager having been appointed to the role on 1st June 2018.

A54.  Rangers' record for the incredible 2020/21 League season was Played 38, Won 32, Drew 6, Lost 0.

A55. Rangers came to Wolverhampton Town for a memorable European semi-final on 19th April 1961.  It was a different era then, with terracing rather than seats, no substitutes allowed and it was even before motorways had been built. Over 10,000 Scottish fans made the trip in the pouring rain. "I stood there all alone, while the boys all down from home sang of Rangers, that team of great renown."

A56. Follow Follow is probably the best known of the Rangers fanzines, and it now has a very solid following online at followfollow.com.

A57. A lion is on the club crest. Unusually for a football club, Rangers have two different official crests. Today the original scroll crest appears on the club's team strips whereas the lion rampant club crest is used by the media and online.

A58. Rangers training facility at Milngavie is known locally as Murray Park after former chairman and owner Sir David Murray, although it also often referred to as Auchenhowie.

A59. Obviously Celtic are Rangers' main rivals.

A60. Although it is considered politically incorrect these days, The Billy Boys is a song that has long been sung by Rangers fans, home and away.

Let's give you some easier questions.

61. What is the traditional colour of the home shirt?
    A. Ice Blue
    B. Navy Blue
    C. Royal Blue

62. What is the traditional colour of the away shirt?
    A. White and Black
    B. White and Blue
    C. White and Red

63. Who is the current club sponsor?
    A. 32Red
    B. Bet365
    C. Betfair

64. Who was the first club sponsor?
    A. McEwan's Lager
    B. CR Smith
    C. NTL

65. Which of these once sponsored the club?
    A. Carling
    B. McEwan's Lager
    C. Tennents

66. Who is the official kit supplier?
    A. Castore

B. Diadora

C. Hummel

67. Who was the club's first foreign signing?
    A. Sean Fallon
    B. Joe Kennaway
    C. Charlie Tully

68. Who was the club's first black player?
    A. Gil Heron
    B. Walter Tull
    C. Mark Walters

69. Who was the club's first match in the league against?
    A. Dumbarton
    B. Heart of Midlothian
    C. Kilmarnock

70. Who started the 2021/22 season as club captain?
    A. Scott Arfield
    B. Connor Goldson
    C. James Tavernier

Here are the answers to the last block of questions.

A61. The traditional colour of the home shirt is Royal Blue. However, as part of knowing the club's history, it is important to know that for the majority of the he first fifty years of the club's existence, the club played in a plain, lighter blue home shirt.

A62. The most common colours of the away shirt are white and red.

A63. Online casino company 32Red is the current shirt sponsor, and has been since 2014.

A64. CR Smith was Rangers' first ever shirt sponsor, back in 1984.

A65. All three of these drinks brands have sponsored the club. Give yourself a bonus point if you knew that.

A66. Castore became the official kit supplier in May 2020 on a five year contract worth a reported £25 million to the club.

A67. Joe Kennaway was the club's first foreign signing back in 1931. He became a dual international playing for both Canada and Scotland.

A68. The club's first black player was Mark Walters who made his debut on 2nd January 1988 in a 2-0 loss at Parkhead.

A69. The 1890/91 season saw the inception of the Scottish Football League, and Rangers were one of the ten original members. Rangers' first ever league match was a 5-2 victory over Heart of Midlothian on 16th August 1890.

A70. James Tavernier started the 2021/22 season as club captain.

Here is the next batch of ten carefully chosen questions.

71. What road is celebrated in an old song?
    A.  Paisley Road East
    B.  Paisley Road North
    C.  Paisley Road West

72. Who was voted Rangers greatest ever foreign player?
    A.  Lorenzo Amoruso
    B.  Stefan Klos
    C.  Brian Laudrup

73. How many times has a Rangers player won the European Golden Boot award?
    A.  1
    B.  2
    C.  3

74. According to the song, what is "The greatest sight I have ever seen?"
    A.  Bonnie Rangers
    B.  A Penny Arcade
    C.  The Blue Sea of Ibrox

75. Where was the legendary Fernando Ricksen born?
    A.  Belgium
    B.  Luxembourg
    C.  The Netherlands

76. What shirt number does Alfredo Morelos wear?
   A. 10
   B. 15
   C. 20

77. Who did Rangers fans vote as the club's greatest ever player in 1999?
   A. Jim Baxter
   B. John Greig
   C. Colin Stein

78. What sport was carried out at Ibrox in the 2014 Commonwealth Games?
   A. Boxing
   B. Rugby Sevens
   C. Wrestling

79. When was the club liquidated?
   A. 2010
   B. 2011
   C. 2012

80. Which of these has played for Rangers and Celtic?
   A. Davie Cooper
   B. Gordon Durie
   C. Kenny Miller

Here is the latest set of answers.

A71. It's an old song, and it's still a goodie. "For when I was a lad I was led by the hand down Paisley Road West. I will never forget that beautiful sight of the red, blue and white. From that day I'd be Rangers for life."

A72. Brian Laudrup signed for the Gers in July 1994 and played a total of 116 goals for the club. He later described his time as "the best four years of my career". His silky skills contributed to him being named SFWA Footballer of the Year twice and he was voted Rangers greatest ever foreign player.

A73. The European Golden Shoe or Golden Boot award is presented to the leading goal-scorer in league matches form the top division of every European national league. Ally McCoist is the only Scottish player to have won the European Golden Boot award. He won it twice, for his 34 goals in the 1991/92 season and also for his 34 goals in the 1992/93 season.

A74. "At Three O'clock Each Saturday, I'll Join The Mighty Throng, With Flags And Banners All Around, I'll Proudly Sing This Song, It's The Blue Blue Blue Sea Of Ibrox, It's The Greatest Sight That I Have Ever Seen."

A75. Fans' favourite Ricksen, who played 182 games for Rangers between 2000 and 2016, was born in The Netherlands.

A76. Morelos wears the number 20 shirt.

A77. In 1999, Rangers fans voted John Greig as "The Greatest Ever Ranger", a title he truly deserves.

A78. Ibrox hosted Rugby Sevens during the 2014 Commonwealth Games.

A79. After a long drawn out process, The Rangers Football Club plc were liquidated on 31st October 2012.

A80. Kenny Miller has played for both Rangers and Celtic.

Here are the next set of European related questions, and let's hope you get most of them right.

81. In what year did Rangers win the European Cup Winners Cup?
   A. 1970
   B. 1971
   C. 1972

82. Who did they beat in the final?
   A. CSKA Moscow
   B. Dynamo Moscow
   C. Spartak Moscow

83. What was the score?
   A. 3-0
   B. 3-1
   C. 3-2

84. Where was the final played?
   A. Barcelona
   B. Berlin
   C. Budapest

85. Who captained the team?
   A. John Greig
   B. Derek Johnstone
   C. Tommy McLean

86. Who was the manager of the team?

A. Walter Smith
B. Willie Waddell
C. Jock Wallace

87. How many of the eleven players in the team were Scottish?
    A. 7
    B. 9
    C. 11

88. What nickname was given to the team?
    A. Barcelona Bears
    B. Barcelona Bobcats
    C. Barcelona Bulls

89. How many major European finals have Rangers reached?
    A. 3
    B. 4
    C. 5

90. When was the last season Rangers competed in the Champions League?
    A. 2009/10
    B. 2010/11
    C. 2011/12

Here are the answers to the last set of questions.

A81. Rangers won the European Cup Winners Cup in 1972, on the 24th May 1972 to be precise.

A82. Rangers beat Dynamo Moscow in the Final.

A83. Rangers won 3-2 with two goals from Willie Johnstone and one from Colin Stein.

A84. The final was played at the Nou Camp Stadium in Barcelona.

A85. The team was captained by John Greig.

A86. It was the legend that is Willie Waddell who led Rangers to victory.

A87. All of the eleven players who played in the 1972 European Cup Winners Cup Final were Scottish.  How times have changed.

A88. They were nicknamed the Barcelona Bears, as the final was played at the Nou Camp Stadium in Barcelona, and the team roared like bears that night.  This was the finest hour in Rangers; silverware strewn history. Disappointment in two previous European finals was forgotten on a very warn evening in Barcelona as the European Cup Winners Cup was finally engraved with Rangers' name and a European trophy was on its way to Govan.

A89. Apart from winning the European Cup Winners Cup in 1972, the club also reached the final in both 1961 and 1967. Additionally the club reached the final of the EUFA Cup in 2008. Rangers were also runners up in the European Super Cup in 1972.

A90. Prior to the 2021/22 season, Rangers last appeared in the Champions League in 2011/12 losing in the 3rd qualifying round to Malmo 1-2 on aggregate. The last time Rangers have appeared in the group stages of the Champions League was during the 2010/11 season.

Here is the final set of questions. Enjoy!

91. What is the club's official twitter account?
    A. @TheGers
    B. @Rangers
    C. @RangersFC

92. How many people died in the 1971 Ibrox disaster?
    A. 55
    B. 66
    C. 77

93. Who was Rangers' first foreign manager?
    A. Dick Advocaat
    B. Pedro Caixinha
    C. Paul Le Guen

94. How many Englishmen have managed Rangers?
    A. 1
    B. 2
    C. 3

95. Who was the last Rangers player to win the PFA Scotland Players' Player of the Year award?
    A. Steven Davis
    B. Paul Gascoigne
    C. James Tavernier

96. Who was the last Rangers player to win the Scottish Football Writers Association Footballer of the Year award?
    A. Carlos Cuellar
    B. Steven Davis
    C. Barry Ferguson

97. How many goals did Derek Johnstone score for Rangers in the league?
    A. 122
    B. 132
    C. 142

98. Who is the current honorary president?
    A. John Bennett
    B. John Greig
    C. Alastair Johnston

99. Who was Rangers' first foreign captain?
    A. Lorenzo Amoruso
    B. Brian Laudrup
    C. Craig Moore

100. What position is Sandy Jardine best known for?
    A. Right Fullback
    B. Right Half
    C. Right Winger

101. Which former legend is honoured with a statue outside the Main Stand?
     A. John Greig
     B. Bob McPhail
     C. Willie Reed

Here is the final set of answers.

A91. @RangersFC is the official twitter account of the club. It tweets multiple times a day, and it has almost a million followers.

A92. The 1971 Ibrox disaster led to 66 deaths and more than 200 injuries.

A93. Dick Advocaat was Rangers' first foreign manager; the Dutchman taking the helm in June 1998.

A94. Just two English men have managed Rangers. Prior to Steven Gerrard, Mark Warburton was the only other English man to have managed Rangers; he was in charge for 82 games from June 2015 to February 2017.

A95. James Tavernier was the last Rangers player to win the PFA Scotland Players' Player of the Year award winning the award at the end of the 2020/21 season.

A96. Steven Davis was the last Rangers player to win the Scottish Football Writers Association Footballer of the Year award, also known as the Scottish Footballer of the Year, winning the award at the end of the incredible 2020/21 season.

A97. Derek Johnstone scored an impressive 132 goals in the league and 212 goals in total for the club.

A98. John Greig is the current honorary president, a role he has held since May 2015.

A99. Brian Laudrup was the first non-British captain of the club. He was captain for 139 days from 1st June 1997 to 18th October 1997.

A100. Sandy Jardine was best known as a right fullback but he did play at wing half and inside forward before manager Will Waddell moved him to fullback. . He was twice player of the year in Scotland and he was a credit to the club being elegant, fast and strong.

A101. It is of course John Greig who has a statue outside the ground. It was unveiled on 2nd January 2001.

That's it. That's a great question to finish with. I hope you enjoyed this book, and I hope you got most of the answers right. I also hope you learnt one or two new things about the club.

If you see anything wrong, or have a general comment, please visit the glowwormpress.com website.

Thanks for reading, and if you did enjoy the book, would you please leave a positive review on Amazon and show your support for this great club.

Come on The Teddy Bears.

Printed in Great Britain
by Amazon

70212539R00028